I0825473

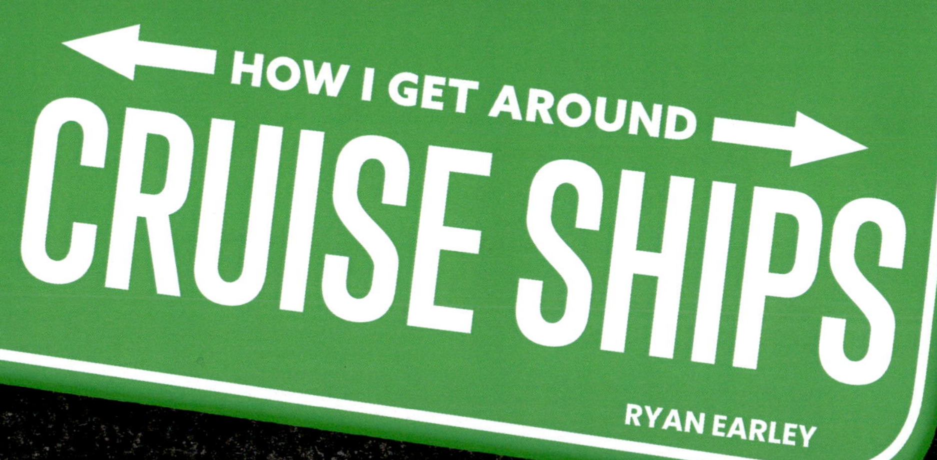

TABLE OF CONTENTS

Sight Words..2

Words to Know....................................3

Index..16

A Pelican Book

Teaching Tips for Caregivers and Teachers:

Research shows that one of the best ways for students to learn a new topic is to read about it.

Before Reading

- Read the title and predict what the book will be about.
- Read the "Words to Know" and discuss the meaning of each word.
- Read the back cover to see what the book is about.

During Reading

- When a student gets to a word that is unknown, ask them to look at the rest of the sentence to find clues to help with the meaning of the unknown word.
- Motivate students with praise and encouragement.

After Reading

- Discuss the main idea of the book.
- Ask students to give one detail that they learned in the book.

Sight Words

all
around
big
by
get
go
have
I
on
some
water

Words to Know

cabins

cruise ship

decks

engines

restaurants

I get around by **cruise ship**.

cruise ship

All cruise ships have big **engines**.

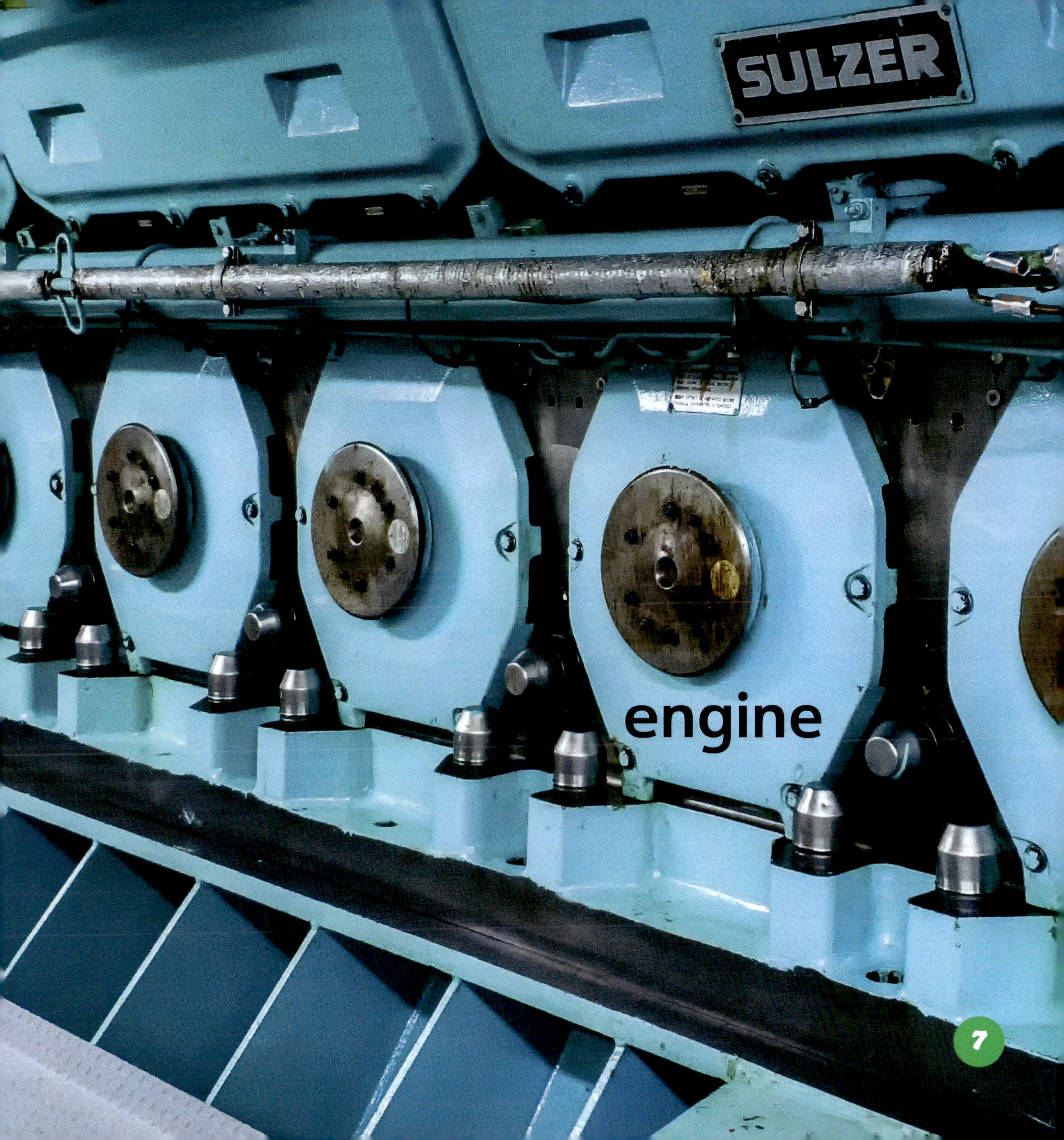

engine

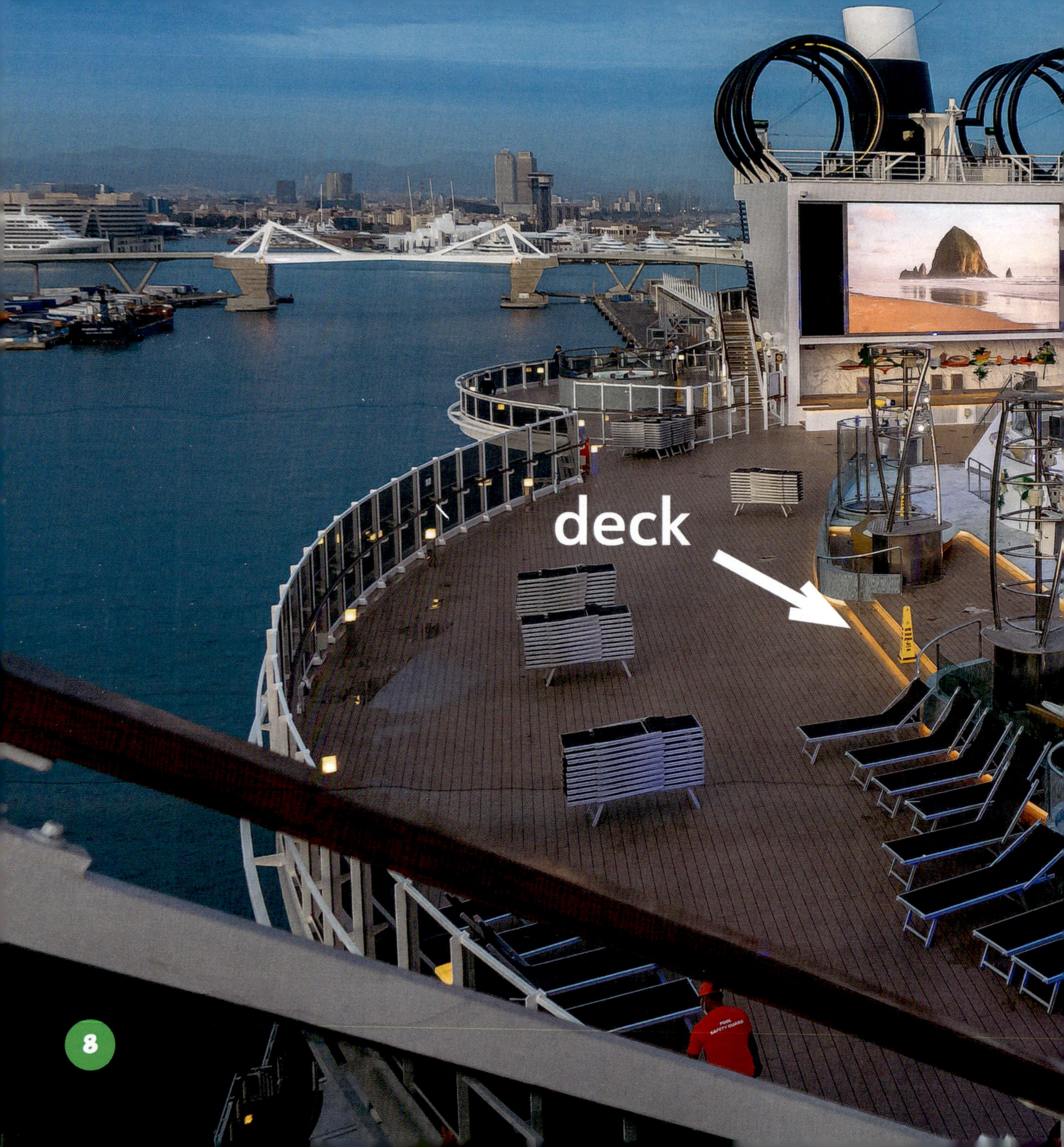
deck

All cruise ships have **decks**.

cabin
WELCOME
KIT

Some decks have **cabins**.

Some decks have **restaurants.**

restaurant

All cruise ships go on water.

Index

cabins 10, 11
decks 8, 9, 11, 12
engines 6, 7
restaurants 12, 13
water 14

Written by: Ryan Earley
Design by: Niko Magaro
Editor: Kim Thompson
Series Development: James Earley

Photos: All images from Shutterstock

Library of Congress PCN Data
Cruise Ships / Ryan Earley
How I Get Around
ISBN 979-8-8945-9263-3(hard cover)
ISBN 979-8-8945-9277-0(paperback)
ISBN 979-8-8945-9305-0(EPUB)
ISBN 979-8-8945-9291-6(eBook)
ISBN 979-8-8945-9319-7(audio)
ISBN 979-8-8945-9333-3(Read-Along)
Library of Congress Control Number: 2024946366

Printed in Canada/012025/CP20250101

Seahorse Publishing Company
seahorsepub.com

Published in the United States
Seahorse Publishing
PO Box 771325
Coral Springs, FL 33077